Unreal Estate

Also by Lyubomir Nikolov:

In English:
Pagan, Carnegie Mellon University Press,
        Pittsburgh, PA 1992
Street, Fakel, Sofia 2005

In Bulgarian:
Summoned by the Tide, Narodna Mladezh, Sofia, 1981
Traveler, Narodna Mladezh, Sofia, 1987
Raven, Anubis, Sofia, 1995
Wasp, Fakel, Sofia, 2005

In German:
Nur ein Steinwurf vom Diesseits das Jenseits, Residenz Verlag,
        Salzburg, Austria, 1993

In Spanish:
Parabolas a medianoche, Ediciones Al Margen,
        La Plata, Argentina, 2006

Unreal Estate

poems by
Lyubomir Nikolov

Translated from the Bulgarian
by Miroslav Nikolov

Carnegie Mellon University Press
Pittsburgh 2009

Acknowledgments

The author and publisher would like to thank the editors of the following publications where some of these poems first appeared:

New European Poets, Modern Poetry in Translation, Sirena, Stand, The World Comes to Iowa, Savremennik, Sega and Trud.

Book design: Elizabeth N. Barsotti

Library of Congress Control Number 2008924382
ISBN 978-0-88748-497-1

Printed and bound in the United States of America

10 9 8 7 6 5 4 3 2 1

"America, a desert with a name . . ."
—Louis Simpson

Contents

Cypresses in Delphi—11

The House—15
Apples—16
Sunday—17
Down There—18
Allegheny Cemetery—19
Wild Goose over the Potomac—20
Sunset—21
Dreaminess—22
In the Dark—23
Melancholy at the End of March—24
Street—25
Sometimes—27
Midnight Parables—28
Water Mill—29
Yard—30
Clouds—31
Fatherhood—32
A Little after Midnight—33
Light—34
Sunflowers—35
Breezewood—36
Hemlock—37

The Blonde in Front of the Museum—41
Fish—42
Saddle River—43
Halved Apple—44
Fire—45
Apis—46
Raspberries—47

Carp—51
Summer—52
Garden—53
Wasps After a Storm—54
Inside—55
The Rose—56
Afternoon—57
Window—58

Petals—61
The Poets of Iowa—62
The Flower Vendor at Judiciary Square—63
On the Missouri—64
Homecoming—65
Snail—66
Fragment—67
Stalactites—68
Old Nebraska Graveyard—69
Counting the Crickets—70
A Cigarette in the Late Afternoon—71
Houses—72

Cypresses in Delphi

I see reason
in the cypresses,
these furled banners.

Any time is good.
Just begin.

I

The House

I'm the master of the empty house.

I enter the bedrooms, lie on the beds,
caress the heavy dressers full of linen,
I savor the perfumes
and bury my beard in the white sheets.

I remove the mirror from the wall.
I wander from room to room
and watch how the other mirrors,
the pink vases and the blue duck in the bathtub
peer into it.

I swig "Barbados" rum straight from the bottle.

I open the windows
and slowly, one by one, set the curtains on fire.
Come.
You'll easily recognize
that red house,
up there on the hill in Highland.

It's ablaze.

Apples

The apples have fallen,
they rot in the yard.
And you aren't here.
Otherwise, everything else goes on as before.
The cricket creaks in the dry grass.
The windowpane is shattered.
A stone lies by the bed.
Shards of glass cover the pillow.

Sunday

Go to the forest.
Chat with the squirrels.
Shake snow from the branches.
And shout.
Shout!

Don't worry.
No one will hear you.

Down There

Something will happen down there

The squirrel, which every morning
grabs a walnut from the neighbor's hand,
is hounded by dogs.

I want to cry out, but I can't.

My mouth is full of straw.
I'm nailed to the stars.

Something will happen down there

Allegheny Cemetery

The marble squirrel
clutching an acorn
will drop it.
The young fog will grow old.
And I, the only one alive
in Allegheny Cemetery this morning,
will get lost among the wet trees.
Who will show me the way
between these low tombs and tall crosses?
A leaf falls from the maple and disappears.
Alice. Jennifer. Scott Macintosh.
Moss blooms in the chiseled names.
The cigarette singes my fingers.
I smother it with my heel.

A breeze. The lake's skin bristles.

Wild Goose over the Potomac

It rained last night in the mountains.
The river swelled with driftwood.
Butterflies circle above the grass
with frayed, muddy wings.

Frogs croak on the flooded banks.
Their bulging eyes glisten.
Herons glide over the river
barely touching the water.

The river flows, cloudy and cold.
I, too, flow beneath uncharted skies.
And the goose, northward bound,
looks like a shattered compass.

Sunset

The sun is setting and fear takes hold of me.
I'm afraid that the loaded carts
will crumble into sounds
and then into whirlwinds of dust.

I'm afraid that time will cease.
That the rabbit, hiding in the clover,
will never leap into the garden
and will die among the stars.

The moon swells with blood.
A scarecrow roams a deserted vineyard.
I fear that the gusts will sweep away
the dandelion on top of the haystack.

Dreaminess

How sweet it is to lie in the darkness
head propped on your fist, eyes half shut,
asking yourself: Is it raining outside,
or are leaves tapping on the window?

Most likely they are leaves.
Large, fiery—dancing in the dark.
For a moment they peer into the room and once more
the wind lifts them high above the ground.

When will this long night end?
The crickets outdoors, when will they stop?
You doze off, and suddenly it dawns on you:
Of loneliness, we die the slowest.

In the Dark

It's good that darkness falls suddenly.
That the visible quickly vanishes.
And the heavens with a massive lid
carefully seal in everything alive.

The night is a hive. Thoughts drone
and pour honey into narrow cells.
Where is the road? A road once passed through here.
Now it winds underground.

In the dark, existence has no aim.
Nests of mud—distant stars fall.
And everything to which you have sworn
betrays you with passion, love and pleasure.

Melancholy at the End of March

You too are a stranger, late sunbeam.
You pierce the clouds, enter through the window
and illuminate the dusty leaves
of the geranium, asleep by the fireplace.
Green flames dance on the ceiling.
The dust is visible. I can feel it,
kiss it with lonely lips
and drink it in with thirsty nostrils.
You will burn out here, drifting sunbeam.
Your life will cease in this room
between the curtains and the empty bed,
among the sounds of falling jazz.
This is the end. The road finishes here.
Who is whistling among the azaleas?
Why is the parrot's belly green?

Street

I wake up and glance out of the window.
Today the sun seems larger.
Dozing in the grass, the cat plays dead. Roses,
legs severed at the knees, bloom in the vase.
What will happen today?
Something always happens. That's time.
To return to the cloud, the dewdrop needs time.
A tear needs time to come back to the eye.
Time for the rain to fall.
The barrel maker, a pencil tucked behind his ear,
needs days
to build the wine's house
and in its eastern wall, high above the spigot, mount a window.
Time for things and people.
Time for the pipes in the cathedral to sound
and for the corn to feed the crows.
Time for the dog with a muzzle of flies
(perhaps killed accidentally by hunters)
lying in the hedge, waiting patiently
for the autumn rain to bear it underground.
One thing's certain: It won't rain today.
Nor tomorrow. Nor next year.
And still, red apples will fall—
fortresses captured by worms.
And how about the house I was born in?
When it starts searching for me with a lantern,
will it remember to look in the well?
Let's say it remembers. Then I'll go inside,
through the keyhole I'll gaze toward the sea.
I'll watch a seagull dragging a rat among the dunes.
Time to this rat, I guess, is a handful of sand.
Silence. And in the silence—a piercing cry.
This is time, space full of intentions and gestures.
An abandoned hearth in which people and trees,
houses and animals, burn with a gentle flame.

Why does the window face the street?
Because the street is time itself. Look:
A truck carrying bails of straw passes by.
A sparrow flies towards a nest in the streetlight,
an endless straw in its beak.

Sometimes

Sometimes objects speak,
revealing that they are alive.

But something must strike them.

Midnight lightning.

Or a thought.

Midnight Parables

The Mercedes plows through the Pittsburgh darkness.
A half-moon in the sky.

"He sent the birds to the moon,
but they returned,
because they had nests and relatives
here, on earth."

Fred lights a cigarette
and coughs.

"A tree complained to Saint Francis:
—I have forgotten what I am.
—Look at the others—replied the Saint.
—Each keeps just a single leaf,
so that come spring, they will remember."

Fred lowers the windows
and points to the roadside trees.

We peer into the night.

Empty nests.
Naked branches.

Water Mill

At night
when the termite
begins to scrape
beneath the bark of the hollow tree
I dream I'm at home.

Not exactly home perhaps,
but in some abandoned mill.

The two rivers flow into one.

The water rushes into the sluice.
Creaking, the wheel starts to turn.

Where is the other millstone?

Yard

Sprawling in the grass, I gaze at the clouds
through branches above my head.
The frost-dusted leaves are doomed.
They cling, but this evening they'll take flight.

What would it be like to sneak into the room
and close the door behind you?
The yellowed leaves look towards the window.
You glance in the mirror and see clouds.

Clouds

White clouds drift by
full of steam and mud.
Where have we come from?
Who made us?

Forgotten, I lie in the grass
chewing a stalk of mugwort.
We've fallen with the dew.
With the dew we'll fade away.

Fatherhood

His head on my pillow my younger son
waves his hand and falls asleep.
"Good night"
still quivering on his lips.
His right knee
touches my chest.
I need some light.
I get up and raise the blinds
a few inches, enough to write:
"Just like that the stars in the sky
cling to one another and don't plummet."

A Little after Midnight

The wind ruffled the roadside tree.

A nightingale called.

The voice came from far away—
as if within the nightingale
sang another nightingale.

Or perhaps within me
another poet eavesdropped,
his ear against mine,

entranced.

Light

Every morning the autumn sun
comes into my attic room.
The three windows face east—
the light enters through them all.
I hear how it treads upon the rug,
and browses through my dusty books.
The sun lights half of the dark door.
A thin ray turns in the keyhole.
I rise and open the windows.
For more light to enter. More. More.

Sunflowers

They follow the sun
stumbling in green clods of dirt,
they get up and walk, walk,

holding their lanterns high.

Breezewood

One hundred miles to Pittsburgh.
One hundred miles to Washington.
God knows how many to Sofia,
I look at the shadows under the dark pines
and cry.

On the back seat of the bus I sob like a virgin.
Pain. And delight.

Delight.

Hemlock

The hemlock's poison
has intoxicated the wasps.
I bend down, inhaling the pollen.
And now my senses whirl.

Young and verdant,
the universe spins around me.
I myself am a universe.
Just like it I'm green.

Gold-crowned churches dance.
A cross spins in the clouds.
And the hemlock wilts.
Strews seeds. And blooms.

II

The Blonde in Front of the Museum

Your bare shoulders sting me like nettle,
little wench.
Your shirt is a slough.
Your body twists and squirms,
trying to slip out of the shirt,
to flow forth onto the pavement.

Never-ending Middle Ages.

I want to loosen the straps.
I want to remove my armor.

Fish

She lies nude on the bed
and smiles.

I bring fish from the tub
and scatter them on the sheets.

They look at me with round, unblinking eyes,
ashamed of their nakedness.

I cover them with orange peel.

Saddle River

Peel another pear,
slice another peach.
Last night fireworks burst like peacock feathers
over the dark meadows.
We drank, celebrating until dawn.
Yet, Independence doesn't mean Liberty.
In the morning I tripped on a fallen nest.
My bare toe sunk into warm down.
A hollyhock was burning in the yard.
A water rat splashed beneath the bridge.
I walked, repeating to myself:
"My boy, we fill the nucleus of the earth."
I'm irradiated. Don't kiss me.
Eat a slice of that bloody peach,
let me suck the stone and go
bury it in the garden.

Halved Apple

The seeds are inside the apple.
The apple is inside the seeds.

Fire

In the fire there is something very feminine,
very warm.
Preparing the twigs and leaves
is like building a nest,
the hands—a cupola
over the small pink flame.
And later,
the air's blazing garment,
the dance,
you'd say that harmonicas are burning—

so many sounds.

Apis

One of his horns is black,
the other—red.

Step out of your clothes, sister,
open the windows wide.

Bathed and fragrant,
tied with a linden thread
the Dead One rides the Apis.

What a divine smile.
What Egyptian calm.

Someone sings.

Green scarabs crawl on the stripped trunk.
A tunic slides off bare shoulders.

Bite me until I bruise. Until I bleed.
I want to wake up.

Raspberries

Raspberries ripen in the garden—
fiery, crimson rubies,
covered in dew.
I pick them with my mouth.

I pluck the moist berries with my tongue.
Juice runs down my chest.
And I sprawl in the thicket
like a gluttonous little beast.

Bearded satyr, innocent child,
with a parched, greedy mouth,
you drank the raspberry venom
and naked, fell asleep under the branches.

In your garden
a snake dances,
biting into a raspberry.

III

Carp

Blood and scales slowly cover the knife.
I grasp it firmly, scraping,
trying not to look the mute creatures in the eye.
I scrape them
as if shaving pig skin—against the grain.
I tear apart their armor,
so that the bodies underneath
will glisten: smooth, soft, naked.
Scales are all over my shirt and pants.
They flit by me like wet husks
hiding my face and my shoes.
And I remember an old icon:
the ravine,
the dragon,
pinned to the ground by St. George's spear,
the pup with a pink tongue
licking the dark clots.
Next to me—a bowl of flour.
I roll the fish.
Blue veins break through the white shirts.
It's noon.
The oil is already hot.

Summer

Nettle, the hardiest flower,
stings my fingers.

Turtles rise from the river,
their ancient shells steam on the rocks.

A dragonfly darts over the water.

The blackberry—a drop of dark honey.

And I, neck drawn out above the grass
am once again a poet.

Garden

For Geo

In the garden, there's always room for a miracle.
Look how they've grown together:
The flower is a rooted butterfly.
The butterfly—a winged flower.

Wasps after a Storm

Drunk with juice and heat
the wasps couldn't fly away.
The storm caught them. The rain
flogged them with green whips.

Now they emerge slowly,
foreheads rammed in the mud.
The murky streams carry
quince blossoms and wings.

With an eye that has rarely cried
you stare at the drenched wasps.
Look, a drop falls from above
and puts out your cigarette.

Inside

If I peer into the window of the black carriage,
I'll see a man with a pipe in his mouth
and slender reins in his lap.
Or a girl
playing with a scarlet leaf
and scribbling in a small book.

A fox barks.
The forest is vermilion
and red.

Perhaps a taxidermist
sits in the carriage
and carefully watches the branches.
He will stop.
A shot will ring out.
Something large and colorful
will tumble down
and decorate the wall for many winters.

No. It's better not to guess.
I must finally approach.

And glance inside.

The Rose

The wind gently rocks it.
A beetle crawls inside
not to get the sweet pollen
but just to swing for a while.

Afternoon

From the curved briar
the spider has crafted a bow.
He has drawn tight an exquisite bowstring
which twangs lightly
when the wind blows.

What will he invent by this evening?
With what other nets and traps
will he try to catch something?

The moment is pliable.

Above the bushes,
above the pine cones in the soft grass,
weighs uncertainty.
As the ancient poet would have said,
from now on everything is possible.

It's afternoon. Evening will fall, then night.
I want to come downstairs at dawn, before the dew,
to see the traps,
to see the spared. And the dead.

I don't know if I'll come.
I'm not quite sure.
I don't know.

Window

I understand the snow—
it doesn't want to fall.

It wants to stay
in the deep
sky.

I understand the leaf.

It doesn't want
to drift
toward the wet grass,
where its brothers rot.

I don't want to look out of the window.

But I look.

I understand the snow—
it doesn't want to fall.

IV

Petals

From the petals
under the bush, the wind
will make another,
even larger rose.

The Poets of Iowa

They always arrive together.
A bunch of hedgehogs
with soft bellies and sharp bristles
on which
the apples of knowledge sway.
They probably come from forests casting golden shadows
because up close they smell of grass and crushed mushrooms.
Dazed, they lie back in green chairs
and their spines crease like the spines of books
filled with the world's unwritten poems.
They are the poets of America's heartland,
who hear the noise of both oceans
like the crack of a bone, broken over a fragile knee.
Brahmins, awaiting summons from Buddha,
trembling for having forgotten his tongue.
I watch them sink into the cornfields.
Startled horses,
they strain their muscles dragging Nothingness.
In the sunset their teeth gleam
like kernels in a cob.

The Flower Vendor at Judiciary Square

The plaza is a laboratory.
We are alchemists.
He changes flowers into money.
I change money into flowers.

On the Missouri

On the bridges of the Missouri
I think about the old men,
the old men with pipes of ancient clay.

In the fog over the Missouri, the old men of my village appear.

They weave nets, play wooden whistles,
by ponds full of crayfish, they sweetly smoke.

They take out flint, steel and tinder
and let me play with fire, too.

Huge sun, sink in the Missouri.
Emerge from the depths, quiet old men.

Homecoming

Next to the house,
among the dahlias and the parsley,
I found my father's shot glass
filled with dirt.

Snail

He always arrives first.
He's the first to crouch in the grass,
there, where blood will spill
and mighty strongholds collapse.

Yes. He's a drunk barbarian.
He sways among the brambles,
peers in the royal chambers
and takes aim at the towers.

Walls topple to the dusty ground.
The weed rains pollen.
His horns raised, he's a slingshot,
a slinger and a stone.

.

Fragment

The mirror shatters.
The shards remain.
The whole is fleeting.
The fragment—eternal.

Stalactites

For Klaus Post

Deep beneath the earth, in the dark,
very slowly,
very timidly,
the elements switch roles.

Stone flows.
Water petrifies.

Old Nebraska Graveyard

The names are barely legible.

The stone has begun to forget.

Counting the Crickets

October. The crickets smell of chrysanthemums.
The sun circles the garden
calling their names
and one by one
they emerge.
Some limp.
Others drag their wings like heavy, muddy trench coats.
Summer is a Waterloo.
I bend down. Turn over a fallen leaf.

Its back is crimson.

A Cigarette in the Late Afternoon

For Tony & Ellen

This morning, for the first time in months,
I heard a bird. I don't know its name. I don't even need to.
It woke up early, filling
its empty summer home with song,
surveying its ephemeral kingdom.
That's how it is. There must always be bounds.
Water, poured into a pitcher
must fill it to the brim, no higher.
The dough in the pan
must rise, but not overflow.
It's the same thing with the song, I guess.
One bird, almost invisible among the branches,
proclaims to its sisters: "My borders end here.
From here on the trees and sky belong to you."
The day wears on. It too has bounds.
The clouds roaming in the sky,
the houses staring at the ground,
the churches tolling for vespers,
coming toward me like a flock from pasture,
with horns of gold and bells on their necks—
everything has limits. And that's fair.
I light my cigarette slowly, with delight,
because even that delight will end eventually,
and I watch how smoke pours from the slender chimneys,
it flows into the sky, warm and sweet.
But the fire is where it belongs. With the ashes.
The chimes ring from the nearby yards.
A plane disappears somewhere behind the mountains.
The tired children return home from school
and I tell myself: It's time for this poem to end
so that something else can begin. I put a period.

Houses

Ruin yourselves, destroy me, houses.
Sink in the snowdrifts.
Tear out your hair of smoke, howl at night,
under the cold moon.

I know how cozy it is beneath the roots.
There, in the mole's caverns.
And like you—peeled and shattered—
I slowly sink towards the dirt.

Ruin yourselves, eaves, chimneys, roofs.
Swing, battered doors.
We will embrace like brothers
under the fallen beams.

Bend over the hungry earth.
Kneel in the mud.
Until one day you break down
into soil and wine, fire and water.